Meeting special needs

A practical guide to support children with
Attention Deficit Hyperactivity Disorder (ADHD)

by Selena Ledgerton

*Dedicated to my father Harry, mother Phyllis
and sister Michelle for all your support.*

*In this book the use of he, him or his is gender neutral and is
intended to include both sexes.*

www.practicalpreschoolbooks.com

Published by Practical Pre-School Books, A Division of MA Education Ltd,
St Jude's Church, Dulwich Road, Herne Hill, London, SE24 0PB Tel. 020 7738 5454
© MA Education Ltd 2007   www.practicalpreschoolbooks.com

Illustrations by Cathy Hughes. Front cover image © iStockphoto.com/Nicole S. Young

Meeting special needs. A practical guide to support children with Attention Deficit Hyperactivity Disorder ISBN: 978-1-904-575-12-2

Contents

Pages to copy and use:

Introduction

The literature available on Attention Deficit Hyperactivity Disorder is huge and you should read as much as possible if you have children with ADHD in your care or in your class.

This is a practical reference guide that aims to help you in your daily work with a child affected by the condition.

Within this book are included the signs and symptoms of ADHD, information on statementing, problems and issues, rewards and boundaries and ideas to help with behaviour and education plans, together with sections on strategies and techniques. These include some holistic approaches and information on coaching.

Behavioural Characteristics

Most behavioural characteristics are apparent at all times. Some children can have issues with attention or concentration, but may not be impulsive or hyperactive.

Any disorder should be identified early to ensure that a child receives the support he needs to attain his full potential. There are numerous problems when diagnosing ADHD, as there are no physical tests available. ADHD symptoms can be masked by other issues such as dyslexia or speech and hearing problems.

Children with ADHD can display few or many of the following symptoms with varying severity:

Hyperactivity

- restlessness or fidgeting;
- inability to sit still for long periods;
- leaving his seat or standing when sitting is expected;
- excessive talking;
- problems in engaging in activities;
- issues with remaining calm;
- running, climbing or explore when it is inappropriate;
- attempting to leave the group or class;

Impulsive behaviour

- easily distracted;
- speaks or shouts during quiet times;
- shouts out answers in class;
- interrupts;
- has problems taking turns;
- spoils games or activities by interfering;
- when upset, may become violent or aggressive;
- acts first and think later, may disregard the safety of others or self-harm;

Inattention

- prone to losing equipment;
- has difficulty focusing on tasks;
- may be forgetful (especially with a long list of instructions);
- easily distracted;
- lack of attention to detail, careless with work;
- reluctant to complete tasks requiring long-term attention;
- finds it difficult to start tasks which require mental effort and be overwhelmed;
- appears not to be listening.

The Question of Restraint

Some children with ADHD can be violent or aggressive. If this is the case, take a course in child-safe restraint, specifically designed for children of the correct age range. This may sound extreme, but it is in the interest of the child and other children in the class.

The ethos of the training is centred on children and child protection. Restraint holds for children are designed to be nurturing and non-aggressive. Many schemes will advise you on how to approach a violent child, as sometimes he will calm down via discussion and an understanding hand on the shoulder. Sometimes the smallest amount of physical contact can have a positive impact.

The child's case worker can advise you on the Local Education Authority's (LEA's) policy regarding such training. You will need written permission from the child's parents saying that you may restrain him if he is a threat to himself or others. Do invite the parents to school and show them the various techniques. They should also be present when you discuss restraint with the child. Reasons for restraint should be explained to the child, who should be reassured that you will only hold him if he tries to harm himself or others. Show him the restraint technique that you will use and ensure that he is comfortable. This way, when you need to restrain the child, he will not be frightened. Explain that you will warn him at any time you intend to restrain.

Restraint is a last resort. When you are trained in restraint you will be advised how to document incidents and will be informed that you should never restrain a child without another staff member being present. In this way the incident can be documented and signed by both you and a witness. Remember, documentation is not just a protection scheme for the child, but also for you. The presence of other staff and the use of thorough documentation are important in case of accusations of abuse. It is virtually impossible to harm a child during restraint if you use the techniques as you were taught. The techniques are there to protect the child.

You will also learn protection procedures for other children in the room and yourself. You may need some form of support after an incident and you will definitely need to take a break. The other children in the class will need support and comfort too, as they may be frightened or upset. They should also be given an appropriate explanation so that they do not resent the child with ADHD.

Resentment and fear can be a major problem in the classroom. If the other children do not understand why a child is acting this way, it can lead to him being isolated or bullied. Once the child with ADHD has recovered from the incident, he should return to the class as soon as possible and a normal routine should be resumed.

A guide through the statementing process

Once a child has been diagnosed with ADHD, he can receive additional funding for one-to-one help in school. He may need behaviour support, equipment or academic help, but to gain the extra funding required he must have a statement of special educational needs (SEN).

This can be a difficult task for staff, parents and child as the process can be both confusing and frustrating. The information here will help you support the family and offer information to teaching assistants, or learning support should they need it.

The 1996 Education Act states that the Local Education Authority has a duty to assess a child who may have SEN and the authority must determine the special educational provision which any learning difficulty he may have calls for, (Section 323).

If assessment shows (under Section 323) that it is necessary for the LEA to determine the special educational provision which any learning difficulty he has calls for, the authority shall make and maintain a statement of his SEN (Section 324-1).

In that statement the LEA must give details of the authority's assessment of the child's SEN and specify the special educational provision to be made for the purpose of meeting those needs (Section 324-2). LEAs have a duty to arrange that the special educational provision specified in the statement is made for the child (Section 324-5).

Once the child is diagnosed (or due to be diagnosed) he can be assessed. Following this assessment, he may receive a statement detailing his special needs and what additional help should be provided. It is then the responsibility of the school and the LEA to organise and fund this help.

Four Steps to a Statement

Under the code of practice for SEN, a child will follow this process. The process should be discussed with the child's parents so they are aware of all the stages.

- *Pre-SEN teacher concerns*. At this stage you should monitor the child and introduce strategies to help him. Information from observations can be documented or an Individual Education Plan (IEP) or Behaviour Plan can be created. These should include targets for the child to achieve and regular review dates.

- *School Action.* If a child does not make progress, you should discuss his issues with the special educational needs coordinator (SENCo). Together you can review the IEP and arrange additional support for the child. The SENCo may choose to observe the child and then organise further help, perhaps in the form of further assessment, different targets or reviews. The LEA may be contacted for further assistance, for example from a behavioural support specialist or adviser.

- *School Action Plus.* The SENCo asks for specialist advice from external services, eg. from a behaviour support specialist or educational psychologist. Based on their findings, parents and headteacher are informed that the child may need to be statemented.

- *Request for a statutory statement.* The LEA looks at the statement request. They decide whether to issue a statement and create one if needed.

The statementing process

Parents have the right to ask the LEA to assess their child for a statement of SEN. The LEA must advise them within six weeks whether or not an assessment will be made.

The parents will need to complete a form and provide examples of the child's behaviour. They must answer all the questions, though they can name a person on the form who can help them. Parents should be advised if your area offers a Parent Partnership Scheme or support network.

If the LEA decides to assess a child, it will ask for reports from: your school, an educational psychologist, the health authority, social services and any other agencies, therapists or professionals involved with the child.

This process can take up to ten weeks. If the LEA decides the child needs a statement, the parents will receive a draft within two weeks. This will summarise the child's educational needs, the type of help needed and how it will be provided.

Parents have fifteen days to consider the draft and respond. They should advise the LEA if there are any changes in circumstances and they can also make additional requests for support or equipment at this point. Changes in circumstances and requests must be supported with evidence from the assessment, along with any further information.

Within eight weeks of receiving the draft statement, the LEA will finalise it. Then it will be reviewed annually. Advise parents to keep all correspondence and store any information you receive in line with data protection procedures.

If the LEA decides not to issue a statement, it must advise the parents of the reasons for this decision. If the parents are not satisfied with the reasons the LEA provides or believe the child's circumstances have changed, they can appeal.

Getting to know you

When first working with a child with ADHD, it is a great idea to use a 'getting to know you' book. It can include all kinds of fun activities and questions for the child to complete.

So much information needs to be gathered at a first meeting, and this book makes it possible for the child to remain occupied and relaxed, while you casually chat to him and gain additional insight.

Here are some

(age, hair
:)

friends

ys
e happy
e sad
e angry
e laugh
ings

Include some multiple choice questions, for example:

I work well when it is quiet/busy/loud
I like to work with a group/a friend/alone

Include any other questions or activities that will be relevant; anything that will help you get to know the child. It is useful to allow the child to update the book each year.

This book shows you the child's likes and dislikes (as well as some emotional triggers) very quickly. He will openly draw what makes him angry and if he ever clams up emotionally or feels vulnerable, you can help him open up or settle him by talking about things he loves. With regard to learning, you can see how literacy, creativity and motor skills are coming along and can even gain insight into how a child sees himself by how he draws his portrait. It is a resource that you can return to again and again. Get involved with the child when he is completing each page, ask questions and record the answers. This is a great bonding exercise and can be very enjoyable as well as useful.

g triggers

ay cause a child
may be having a
rates or
upsets him.

Some children may be triggered by noise, some may find a long session difficult. You must get to know your child and learn through observation and documentation what it is that triggers his behaviour.

Information on triggers is invaluable when writing the child's IEP. Sessions and support can be tailored to avoid triggers as much as possible without isolating the child from the class. Use some of the child's triggers to introduce relaxation or anger management techniques; these can be added to the IEP as goals.

For Example:

• John finds maths difficult and becomes easily frustrated if he gets stuck. He will then leave his seat and begin to disrupt the class;

• John is told that if he gets stuck, he should come and write the sum on the

whiteboard right away and we can work on it together;

• John will receive a sticker for his chart if he does not disrupt the class during this session.

This may seem simple. John becomes distracted, and possibly hyperactive, when frustrated. He feels overwhelmed because he cannot complete the problem and if you are helping another child, he is stuck in his seat with nothing but his book. You are taking away his frustration by allowing him to leave his seat and walk away from his book.

He can move around and use up some excess energy, as he would when he is disruptive, but he now has a goal and provides you with a physical signal that he needs help. The whiteboard also offers him a different medium to work with, which will help prevent boredom. John is offered a sticker if he doesn't disrupt the class, because if he were offered a sticker for writing a sum on the board, every sum would be on the board.

It is important that the child is permitted to move. One of the most common triggers for a child with ADHD is losing face with his peers or being singled out. He may leave his table and go to the whiteboard, as long as he sticks to his goal.

Working with parents

All parents are different. Some fight for their child's rights, some find ADHD overwhelming and have trouble coping. No matter what their outlook, they all love their child and want to act in his interest.

It is your responsibility to keep parents informed of everything that is going on. You can keep them up to date, explain the statementing process to them and support them through it. It is important to encourage them to work with you. Parents can feel socially isolated for a range of reasons: the child's behaviour outside school may have caused arguments with neighbours or friends, and some parents may even isolate themselves as they try so hard to spend time with their child. It can be a confusing time and many parents feel lonely and depressed.

By making parents an integral part of the child's school life, you can give them a sense of control and understanding, which can be empowering. Include them in meetings, so they are aware of the child's goals, and be willing to take their advice. They can provide vital information that may help identify triggers and share strategies that have worked for them. The majority of contact with parents of a child with ADHD may be for negative reasons. This can be very disheartening for them, so make the effort to inform them of all of the positives too. Then the parents can talk to the child about his achievements at home and encourage him at the start of each day.

Introduce a daily communication book for parents. You can note both positives and negatives through the day, and any rewards or boundaries. The parents can use this to let you know how the child responded to homework or if he has had a good morning before school. If a child has had an argument or outburst before school, this can affect the child's behaviour throughout the day.

If you know that the child may be upset, you can provide an opportunity for him to calm down and talk to him before any structured lessons. Without the book, you may not understand why the child is angry. It can also be used to notify parents of meetings or ask them to come in to see you. When you are writing the child's IEP, talk to the parents about it. Advise them of the child's different goals and introduce them to his reward scheme. Encourage the parents to introduce similar strategies at home to give the child structure, routine and a unified approach. Parents usually appreciate reward schemes at home, as they can offer much better incentives than you can at school.

What a child needs

Structure

Children with ADHD really need structure. Guidelines, rules and routine form structure, whereas differentiation relates to the curriculum with regard to content, style and delivery. When working with a child with ADHD, you must be flexible with both.

Areas of the curriculum are adapted for most children, but for children with ADHD changes may need to be made on the spot (usually depending on their reaction to the session). Constant revision may be needed day-by-day. This may seem a tall order, but with various structures in place it can be achieved relatively easily.

Many children with ADHD do not like change and are easily bored. You need to provide a regular timetable that provides stability and security so they are aware of their weekly routine. This must be combined with interesting sessions to whet their appetite at the start of the day. Be sure to tell them all the wonderful things you will be doing.

You can introduce a golden rule sheet. These rules are for the whole class, and the sheet can be created during circle time by asking the children what the rules should be. You can make suggestions too, to ensure all the rules are covered, such as turn taking, not leaving your seat, disruption, violence and taking care of property. Do include everything you wish as this will be very useful later on.

With regard to your classroom, allocate specific areas and make sure the children are aware of them.

These areas can include a role-play area, a reading corner and an art station. Include a writing desk with postcards and notepaper, a cool-down zone and PC table. These different areas can be very useful if a child is finding a task difficult and needs a break or if you need to alter a task so that a child can complete it. A child must be made aware of which areas of the classroom are accessible at different times. If an ADHD child completes his work, it is difficult to sit in his seat with nothing to do. With these structured areas in place you can direct him to one of the activities or even let him choose one. Don't forget, this is a class-wide strategy.

You should also consider seating and storage. Most children are protective of their own things, though a child with ADHD can be overly-protective. It all depends on a specific child's triggers and how he reacts. Children with ADHD already feel 'different' and it is your mission to dispel that. The advantage of a structured classroom is that it is class-wide. All the children have the same experience, which supports inclusion. You are not separating the child with ADHD nor are you making him feel different. Allocate a seat to each child with his name on it and include 'do not touch other children's property without permission' on your golden rule sheet. If you introduce a behaviour and reward scheme in class, explain the process to the whole class and include all the children in the scheme.

The structure of the class also relates to your expectations, so make the details of the scheme clear and state why children may receive a reward or a punishment. These expectations must be consistent. The children can be referred to the rule sheet and can understand the consequence of any errors. The same applies to rewards. Children with ADHD should be given on-the-spot rewards and praise as they have little response to long-term rewards. This can cause resentment from children who do understand long-term rewards. Although rewards are positive, again an ADHD child can feel singled out if you treat him differently. Try to treat all the children in the same way, but feel free to vary the rewards. One day you may wish to offer extra playtime (in minutes), another day you may choose to give stickers or time on the PC. If you use a merit point or sticker system with a reward

for reaching a certain target, it defeats the object when you are constantly giving stickers out. Mark which days the children can earn stickers on the class timetable, when they can earn time on the PC and when they can earn extra playtime. Advise them that fantastic behaviour could mean a bonus sticker, even when it is not a sticker day.

Finally, there are whole-school structures to consider. Ensure that your class knows the school rules and pays special attention to punctuality, as this can be a problem for children with ADHD. Put a wipe-clean sheet on the wall with all of the children's names on, and as each child walks into class they can mark themselves off. When they have five symbols for the week, they get a sticker which contributes to their long-term reward. Another approach is to offer the chance to earn some free time for the class at the end of the week in exchange for five punctual days from all the children. It is important not just to reward or punish for punctuality, but explain its importance. Tell the children that if they are late, the whole class has to wait for them. In addition, there are great things that you might have planned that there would not be time to do. Encourage the children to make it a group effort. You may be surprised by the results.

If your school has a uniform or dress code, point out when a child looks particularly smart. This can instil a sense of pride throughout the class and encourage the children to take care of their uniforms. Children with ADHD can have a problem with uniforms as they may refuse to wear it. A uniform is symbolic and if a child is having problems at school he may reject it. Many parents have been forced to spend a fortune on replacement items, as due to their child's hyperactivity and behaviour his uniform is ruined within weeks. Encouragement from you and praise for looking smart can only reap positive results. After all, you are a role model and the class teacher; you may find the children will try their best to look smart in the hope that you will acknowledge their effort. Complimenting them will raise self-esteem and encourage them to take pride in themselves.

To avoid a shock reaction or fear, you should make sure all the children know about fire exits and fire drill. Hold your own drill every week and let the children take turns in making the noise of a bell.

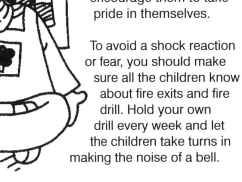

Lapses in behaviour are more likely when the class' structure is broken. A child may have to leave the class to go to another; he may run an errand or go on a field-trip. He could be just going to lunch or playing outside. For children with ADHD, there must be structure everywhere and they need to be aware of how you expect them to behave. If you don't tell them when there are new expectations, they can become very confused or frustrated.

Here are a few ideas:

- if a child has violent tendencies or anger issues, he should be supervised unobtrusively during play;
- step-by-step playtime procedures should be displayed and practised;
- lunchtimes should have structure too. If necessary, allocate times for visiting the toilet, washing, eating lunch and play. Ensure all the children and lunchtime staff are aware of this;
- minimise movement from one class to another;
- advise children of your expectations and safety precautions if they are going on a field-trip;
- practise lining up single-file and in pairs whenever possible;
- encourage the children to walk sensibly when moving around school and explain why (health and safety, wet floors, bumping into others, accidents);
- wherever children go, remind them of your expectations and how they should behave. Offer a reward if a child acts responsibly.

Field-trips are an integral part of school life. Children with ADHD should not be excluded unless behaviour problems are extreme. Complete a risk assessment and ensure that staff-to-child ratios are high. Field-trips with instructors and organised activities are preferable to sightseeing, which can be chaotic. You should also notify the parents (in case they wish to attend) and inform the child of your expectations, any boundaries and health and safety procedures. Remember to document the trip in your observations book and take any medication the child needs with you. Follow school procedure when taking medication off the premises.

A school which understands learning styles

Many schools have expectations for learning that are not realistic for a child with ADHD. For example: being a good listener, focusing on task, exhibiting appropriate behaviour, being able to work independently and working quietly.

Fortunately many schools are now altering their expectations to support children's learning and accommodate their personal learning styles. When working with a child with ADHD, it is important to know your child's learning style. By examining the learning styles a child rejects or ignores, you may be able to flag possible triggers or identify areas in which the child can improve.

If a child is a visual or kinaesthetic learner, he will probably not enjoy writing for long periods. You can encourage writing by allowing the child to write a short piece and design a beautiful border or draw a picture afterwards. This will help develop a learning style he doesn't use (writing) and will allow him to nurture his own style (drawing). You should also be aware that some children have mixed learning styles. The majority of children with ADHD tend to be visual and kinaesthetic learners, though some respond well to audio tapes.

Some common characteristics of these learning styles are:

Visual learners

- learn best by looking and observing;
- appreciate posters, overhead and colours;
- respond to presentations including video, film and television;
- want to see how things are done;
- love drawing, painting and doodling;
- appreciate PC work and visuals;
- like the interactive whiteboard;
- work well with diagrams (eg, mind maps);
- can visualise well;

Auditory learners

- learn well by listening and speaking;
- learn from audiotapes;
- enjoy rhythm, rhyme and poetry;
- can discriminate sounds;
- respond to auditory learning and reading strategies;
- learn languages easily;

Kinaesthetic learners

- can create and like to make things;
- enjoy dismantling and rebuilding;
- use their hands and whole bodies to learn;
- like movement;
- are interested in how things work;
- use their feelings;

Print learners

- show good reading comprehension;
- read to learn and for pleasure;
- write stories and poetry;
- have good imagination;
- write well and write for pleasure;

Interactive learners

- learn via discussion and dialogue;
- are able to lead;
- can be followers;
- are social and approachable;
- appreciate group work and co-operative learning.

A child with emotional and behavioural disorders, learning difficulties or special needs may veer towards one specific learning style. This may be because he is highly creative, prefers reading stories and books or may be a computer whiz. We must utilise each child's learning style to create interesting and enjoyable lessons. We must also include elements from other learning styles to show a child that he can learn in different ways and enjoy other elements (reading, writing, auditory). Some practitioners teach in a way that only complements their own learning style. This may be why a child responds well to one teacher, but not to another.

It is no surprise that children with ADHD tend to be kinaesthetic or visual learners. Visual learners respond to imagery, presentations, colour and art - all exciting, interesting elements. Kinaesthetic learners are naturally inquisitive. They want to know everything about an object or process and like to experiment, move and play to learn.

Children who have ADHD and are visual learners not only feel restricted by lessons that don't nurture their learning style, but can also become frustrated and even enraged by this without explanation. If a lesson is not offered where they can move, this both restricts their learning style and makes them frustrated as they have no outlet to use up excess energy. Confused and frustrated, they may become angry or tearful at school or when they get home, and no-one can understand why.

Visual techniques are pretty obvious. Anything that stimulates the mind through imagery, interaction, drawing and colour can be used. Many children are kinaesthetic learners with some elements of visual learning and it is simple to create interesting lessons that nurture this style.

All sessions should include some form

of movement. You could suggest swapping groups every fifteen minutes to share ideas or discuss a problem. Take the children outside for an activity or get them involved when you are explaining the session. Instead of drawing three dots on the board, bring up three children. For counting or times tables you can hang a clothesline in the class and have the children peg the numbers in the correct order, or rather than explaining history or science, let the children be the characters or elements. During story time introduce costumes and props and let the children take on characters and act out the tale. Get them moving and have fun.

When learning to write, kinaesthetic learners do not respond well to a paper and pen. They need to move and an activity that feels like play is much easier to remember. Try sand trays. Place some coloured sand in a shallow tray and the children can draw their letters or words in the sand (this is useful for tactile learners too). If you need to record their work you can take digital photos. This is great for making name cards when children write their names for the first time. For younger children you can dim the lights and use a torch. For spelling, use floating letters in water. Older children can experiment with different media. They can type up their work on the computer, create a large poster, a book that needs photographs and PC research or they can turn their story into a play and act it out.

Understanding staff and parents

Both teaching staff and parents can work together to support a child with ADHD and demonstrate a mutual respect for each others' efforts.

All school staff want to nurture a child's learning and then send him home happy, positive and fulfilled. It is more likely that when he leaves school happy, he will have a positive night. Parents have a similar responsibility. Morning routines should be as stress-free as possible, so the child can come to school happy and ready to learn. A regular routine with no surprises will help.

When teaching and caring for a child with ADHD, parents and teachers should:

- stay calm and positive;
- encourage the child and give him consistent rewards and feedback;
- have a positive behaviour policy so the child realises good behaviour draws attention. Reward good behaviour and ignore any harmless poor behaviour;
- have consequences in place for poor behaviour and explain the positives of correlating good behaviour;
- be knowledgeable about ADHD, its symptoms, possible behaviours;
- be aware of medications, side effects and safety procedures;
- ensure the child has structure and routine;
- stick to the rules;

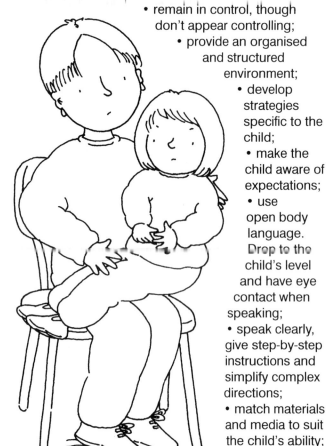

- remain in control, though don't appear controlling;
- provide an organised and structured environment;
- develop strategies specific to the child;
- make the child aware of expectations;
- use open body language. Drop to the child's level and have eye contact when speaking;
- speak clearly, give step-by-step instructions and simplify complex directions;
- match materials and media to suit the child's ability;

- ensure the child understands instructions before starting a task;
- advise all the children what to do if they need help;
- introduce a parent-teacher communication book for contact, noting incidents, rewards and homework;
- be prepared to give extra time to finish work;
- give the child space if his frustration or anger is about to peak;
- add interesting fun elements to formal tasks in line with learning styles;
- criticise the behaviour, not the child. Say "this behaviour" not "your behaviour";
- be willing to adapt activities and lessons to the child's learning style;
- be prepared to change strategies if they are not working after a set time;
- offer discreet signals so the child can alert you without being singled out;
- keep things in perspective;
- set appropriate homework. A child with ADHD may work more slowly than other children, so takes twice as long;
- take a child-safe restraint course if necessary;
- have a sense of humour and be prepared to admit when you are wrong;
- coach and praise the child for good work and behaviour, encourage emotional discussion whenever possible and verbalise your own feelings to set an example.

If the child has a negative day, note down any circumstances in your observations to help you understand and identify any triggers. Include time, day, activity, subject and what the child was asked to do. It is also an idea to note the temperature, if the child was hungry or tired and if they had any problems prior to the session. Remember, children with ADHD respond to change, so document any changes to the classroom or absences (including staff).

Parents may need help caring for an ADHD child or with other problems. Print off a list of useful contacts for them in your area. This could include counsellors, social services, psychologists and information on benefits and support groups. If they come to you for help, reassure them. Never criticise or change what they are doing as this can undermine and upset them. If you need to advise the child's parents, you should discuss new techniques that they can introduce and let them make suggestions too. Remember to praise them for all the work they have already done. If they ask for further help, it is best to direct them to the child's psychologist or a counsellor.

Your LEA will have a list of support groups and contacts.

A supportive environment

Classroom layout is important. It is a good idea to seat a child with ADHD close to the teacher's desk, but within the class group. Position him at a table where he can face you and where there are not too many other children. Children on the same table should be good role models, who are supportive and prone to peer tutoring. Introduce a buddy system, so that each child has a buddy on his table who he can ask for help. Encourage the child with ADHD to help children too; he is well able to do so. Avoid distractions. If a child constantly fidgets or taps, offer something he can use to occupy his hands. Finally, offer a chill-out zone or quiet place where a child can relax and invite him to bring something from home to comfort and calm him when he is there.

Having a PC available can be highly beneficial when working with a child with ADHD. It offers a multi-sensory experience, it is suitable for visual, auditory and kinaesthetic learners and it can be challenging. Children see the PC as a game, so it holds their focus and they control the action and the pace. Surprisingly, as an inanimate object the PC can help a child with ADHD emotionally too. The PC does not shout if you make a mistake and it is relatively unrestrictive and forgiving. Work can be corrected before printing (many children with ADHD become frustrated if their work looks messy compared to others).

For creative children the PC is a wonder. Not only can they draw, but they can upload photographs and videos, hear sounds and play with music. Ensure that PC times are allocated. A child with ADHD can easily become dependent on this little box and in no way is it a substitute teacher. PCs should be presented as both a treat and a tool, to be used at the appropriate time.

The hall can be a difficult environment for a child with ADHD. Assemblies can require children to sit quietly for long periods. Some assemblies are relatively short and time is broken up with singing and music, so that many children with ADHD can cope. For those who can't, you have to be realistic. By taking them into assemblies for long periods you are setting them up to fail, which can only upset them as they know

their limitations. Sometimes a little goes a long way. Initially, the child should attend the important parts of an assembly, so he doesn't have to sit for too long. He may cope better if he has a role in the assembly. Some children cannot cope with assemblies at all. If the strategies above are unsuccessful, provision may need to be made for them in another class during assembly. If this happens, record the assembly on audio tape. This can be played during a quiet lesson so the child does not feel excluded.

Staff on playtime duty should be aware that a child has ADHD. You may wish to advise supervising staff of your reward scheme too, so they can continue this outside and reward sensible play. The playground should be a place for freedom and expression. The child can play games and run around, which can burn off extra energy. There are just a few precautions. if the child has anger issues or violent tendencies, observe him unobtrusively.

Ask playtime staff to notify you if there are any signs that the child is being bullied or is lonely or distant.

Children with a record of absconding must be supervised. During PE or when you are on duty, introduce some old-fashioned team games to the children to encourage them all to exercise and work together. These games can also promote inclusion and can help if the child is feeling isolated.

All the precautions listed for playtime should also be considered during PE. A child with ADHD always needs structure, but never more so than during physical education and play as there are more dangers to consider. Introduce a routine. Line up the children before each physical activity and at the start and end of play. Allocate PE games and activities to specific groups and develop turn-taking skills as each group swaps over. Encourage the children to have fun and to take care of each other.

Strategies for working

Remember that every child is different. Strategies listed here include behaviour strategies, lesson ideas based on learning styles and observations that may help. Remember to note any strategies you use in your observations, as well on the child's IEP or IBP.

Class work

In literacy, a child with ADHD may have numerous problems, so it is important to provide the basics before going any further. Spelling, handwriting and reading can all be issues, along with a lack of comprehension and possible disinterest in the subject. Skills like pen grip, letter formation and size should be mastered, as children can become frustrated by messy handwriting, errors or being unable to finish because they work slowly.

Once they can work confidently, introduce interesting tasks which embrace their learning style. Questions and Answers sessions can be answered verbally sometimes, rather than having to write answers down, and if children are writing, allow them additional time to finish their work. Literacy can be fun and interesting. Instead of writing a story, introduce play-writing and allow each group to act its play out for you, or offer a choice of activities with the same theme. Children could write a travel story, write a postcard or make a travel advert (all of which should include drawing). When working with a child with ADHD, you should also be willing to adapt the work set.

The computer can help with reading. Story software is readily available. It is vital to make the child realise that literacy is not just boring reading and writing. It can be fun.

Some children with ADHD can also have dyslexia or dyspraxia, which affect literacy. If this is the case, it is best to speak to their psychologist for advice and add any strategies and instructions to the child's IEP.

A great way for children to experience a story is to be part of it. Try introducing audience participation and sound effects when telling a story. Tell the children that you will start off the sounds when they are needed. This encourages them to listen quietly and then take part at an appropriate time. Storytime can be multi-media too. There are many interactive fairy tales on the internet and software is also available for the PC. Make sure you monitor the story beforehand, set up security controls and supervise the children if you choose to use the internet. Then you will be working in line with child protection procedures.

it is important to offer sessions that include movement, interaction and colour. Use lots of verbal communication, flash cards and maths games. Have a washing line with numbered cards for times tables and counting. Introduce numbered (netball style) bibs, so the children are human flashcards. Grids can be taped on the floor and the children can dress up as pirates and find the treasure box. Anything is possible and it can only encourage all your children to learn and draw the interest of a child with ADHD.

Many children with ADHD are good at maths because of their special learning skills. Memory issues can cause problems, so be sure to revisit and repeat as much as you can. It is handy to use flashcards and worksheets to aid memory. Children with ADHD can become frustrated when mathematical questions are asked in sentences or if there are multiple ways to answer a question. When questions are presented in words, suggest they pick out the numbers and draw the sum. Let them choose the technique they prefer to work something out, or go through new techniques stage by stage to avoid confusion and frustration.

All other subjects should be approached in the same way as literacy and numeracy. Make sessions as interactive and interesting as possible, use verbal communication when you can, introduce music to the class, get the children moving and offer different media. Give the children a choice of activities and lift their self-esteem with praise. Remember that you can improve on any activity with a bit of thinking outside the box.

If you need some inspiration for PE, here are a few fun suggestions:

Rainbow Hoops
Place different coloured hoops on the playground and turn your back. The children run around until you shout 'hoops' and must choose a coloured hoop to stand in. Call out a colour and the children in that hoop are 'out'. Some practitioners prefer to avoid games where children are 'out', as waiting on the sidelines can cause a child with ADHD to feel frustrated. But I feel that they help to teach turn-taking and patience. These games are perfectly possible if you avoid the word 'out' and the children leaving the game become cheerleaders.

Ball Relay
This can make the child feel part of a team and does not have many instructions. Children stand in lines of five with legs apart, the child at the front has a basketball. The children must pass the ball from front

to back through their legs and when the child at the back of the line gets the ball, he runs to the front of the line. Now the children must pass the ball to the back over their heads. Again the child at the back runs to the front. This continues, legs then arms, until the child who started the game is back at the front. The team that finishes first, wins.

Beans

This is a great game for exercise and memory. The children walk around and wait for you to call out an instruction. If you call:

Runner Beans!	They run around.
Jelly Beans!	They wibble-wobble like a jelly.
Chilli Beans!	They pretend to be cold.
Broad Beans!	They make themselves as wide as possible.
French Beans!	They shout 'Bonjour!'
Jumping Beans!	They hop or jump.
Baked Beans!	They lie on the floor and sunbathe.
Frozen Beans!	They freeze like statues.
Beany Baby!	They pretend to cry.
Tinned Beans!	They huddle together.
Magic Beans!	They pretend to cast spells.
String Beans!	They lie on the floor and make themselves as long as possible,

The great thing about this game is that if the child with ADHD has memory problems he can be helped by his peers to remember. No-one is 'out' in this game, it is just fun.

With regard to science, PE and baking (for example) your priority should be safety. Tell the children what can happen and how it can be prevented, advise them of any relevant school procedures and have structures in place to ensure their safety. Look at your lesson and do your own risk assessment. Remember children with ADHD can be both inquisitive and ingenious, so be prepared for all eventualities.

There are numerous story books available that relate to children with ADHD. By reading these stories to the class you can encourage understanding and make the child feel more at ease. Two useful books are:

Shelley, the Hyperactive Turtle by Deborah Moss is the story of a bright young turtle who is not like other turtles (age 3-8).
Eukee the Jumpy, Jumpy Elephant by Clifford L. Corman is about a hyperactive elephant who moves through the jungle like a tornado, unable to pay attention like the other elephants. He begins to feel sad, but gets help after a visit to the doctor.

Language is very important when working with children with ADHD. Be sure to address the behaviour and not the child, as this can diminish their self-esteem. Say "this behaviour is causing harm" rather than "you hurt him!".

If the child has difficulty remaining on task you may wish to offer him a quiet space to work, a buddy to work with or the option of completing the work on the computer. You could play relaxing music during class sessions or offer the child headphones so he can listen to music if it aids concentration. If the child will not take responsibility for his actions or an argument, it is best not to force him to speak. Avoid arguing with him and remain calm, but guide him to the time-out area to cool down. Discuss the incident later when the child is calm, and agree on a consequence.

When working on the carpet or as a whole class, try introducing discussion times. It can be difficult for a child with ADHD to sit for long periods without moving or speaking. When introducing the session, provide an opportunity for the children to discuss their ideas, come up with an answer or suggest an activity. Use an egg timer so the children know when discussion time is over. This will allow a child with ADHD to speak when he would normally feel restricted. If you introduce legitimised speech, you may also want to offer legitimised movement. If a child with ADHD feels his frustration is escalating, he should be able to do something about it. Advise the child that whenever he feels that way, he can walk to the chill-out zone (he doesn't need to ask).

Do not let children pick teams. This is an important point. Children with ADHD do not like to be singled out, as they can get very upset because they were last to be picked, but sadly it happens. It is heartbreaking for the children, it can isolate them and they can refuse to play or become distant. You can choose teams or perhaps use literacy or numeracy groups that the children know already.

If a child with ADHD is bored he can become fidgety and possibly disruptive. It is important to nip boredom in the bud. Tell the children where they can go in the class on completion of their work and reward any child you see waiting patiently for your help. This will help a child with ADHD understand that he will receive positive attention if he is patient. If he is bored there is a choice of activities.

Encourage a child with ADHD to tell you how he is feeling. If this is difficult, introduce a discreet sign or signal he can give when he feels tense or upset. As the child's emotional literacy improves, this can then be developed into a self-monitoring system where the child recognises stress and administers taught relaxation techniques.

Use as many different media as possible, as this keeps things interesting. Have the children write answers on whiteboards and hold them up, use the children as props and get them moving, use an interactive whiteboard, the computer, books, images, photos, go outside, use sand, modelling clay, bricks, papier-mâché, drawings, anything and everything you can.

Brain Gym is a wonderful system of exercises that children can complete before a session. These exercises draw oxygen to the brain, encourage concentration and get the children moving - all positive elements for a child with ADHD. Exercises include rubbing your tummy and patting your head, one hand touching the opposite knee, closing your eyes and touching your nose and many more.

Healthy eating. Educate your children about healthy eating and remind them whenever possible. Children who are already hyperactive will suffer with an overload of sugar and E numbers. Keep an eye on their eating habits and if you are concerned, discuss it with their parents.

Use your observations, discussions and the 'getting to know you' book to get to know your child. If his behaviour begins to deteriorate and he refuses to calm down or use the chill-out zone, distract him from his behaviour by talking about something he loves or enjoys. You can even try making him laugh. You only need a smile from the child and his frustration subsides.

Bosom buddies – Not! Although it is tempting to encourage children with ADHD to make friends, they should be left to build their own relationships. A nudge in the right direction is fine, but friendships cannot be forced and children may become resentful if you try to push.

Memory, fiddling and interruptions. It is very common for a child with ADHD to forget a list of

instructions. Use mind maps, diagrams or written instructions when you can and provide information in manageable chunks. Offer a squeezy toy or paper and pen if a child fiddles during quiet time. Giving him something to do with his hands can help him focus on you.

If a child with ADHD is constantly interrupting the class, there are some strategies you can try. Two good ones are 'wait for a gap' and 'here is my list'. Before sitting in a group, discuss the 'wait for a gap' technique with the child. Explain that he will receive praise if he waits for a quiet moment before he speaks and a sticker if he puts his hand up. With 'here is my list' the child writes down what he wants to say and can draw a shape of his choice. This prevents him interrupting though he can still present you with his ideas after you have finished speaking to the group.

Lead by example. The way you act and respond to a child with ADHD is how other children will respond too. If you are encouraging and supportive the children will mirror that behaviour. Initially other children in the class may reject the child with ADHD as they do not understand him. If you are non-aggressive and calm, they will be too. This is one reason why ignoring minor disruptions is important.

The other children will copy that behaviour and the child with ADHD will come to understand that they get little attention from behaving inappropriately. If the child with ADHD is patient or courteous and is rewarded, the children will pick up on that too and offer praise. They will embody your generosity and

Case Study

become one of the best support strategies you have. Praise your children whenever you can.

While working with *James (a child with ADHD), I used observation and discussion to find ways to help. When frustrated, James would throw things, push other children around and run off and hide in a quiet place. He would show little remorse for his actions. James loved writing (which is unusual) and after talking to him about his behaviour. I introduced a diary for him to write down his thoughts and feelings.

He could also write about his emotions and the problems that he had. By physically writing down the things he had done and how he felt, he began to realise

that he was harming others and started to show remorse and apologise. We also introduced a chill out zone and anger management/relaxation strategies. If he felt frustrated he would count down from ten and breathe deeply. If he felt his frustration was escalating he could walk to his chill-out zone immediately (without needing to ask). This eliminated the majority of his outbursts and he stopped running off completely as he had a quiet place to go. James became much happier in class and was able to build friendships with the other children.

Jennie Palmer B.Ed, Oliver Plunketts Primary School / Glazebury Primary School, Warrington, Cheshire.
* Child's name changed.

Emotional Literacy

A child's ability to learn relies on his ability to manage personal and social tasks. If he can't understand and express his emotions and needs, his work will suffer. To build relationships children also need to be aware of others, what they are feeling and how to communicate.

For children with ADHD, self-esteem is a big issue. Frustration builds up when they cannot complete a task or it is too overwhelming, and this makes them feel like failures. Relationships with others may also be difficult as they can feel isolated, different or misunderstood because of their disorder.

Children can benefit greatly when they understand their emotions and feelings. It is a skill to be able to share your emotions and convey them to others. Many children find this very difficult as they are self-aware and don't want to sound silly in front of their friends. This can be overcome if Emotional Literacy is used as a class-wide strategy. If it is introduced and everybody does it, it will soon become commonplace.

Discussing feelings can begin at circle time. The children can take a 'smiley face' card or 'sad face' card from the centre of the circle and talk about a time they felt happy or sad. As time goes on, new faces expressing different emotions can be introduced to the pack.

An important time to use Emotional Literacy is when two children argue or disagree. Ask children to "take turns and use your words please". The technique works well, even in nursery. Use a bear as a turn-taking tool. The child holding it says what happened and how he is feeling. He passes it to the other child so that he can have his turn. Emotional Literacy is also about teaching how to resolve issues, so help the children be good listeners and when the turn-taking has ended ask "how can we fix this problem?" When working with children with ADHD, Emotional Literacy can play a significant part in achieving goals.

Children begin to understand that they can share how they feel and express what causes them to be frustrated and unhappy, and most importantly that someone will listen. They become more expressive and can ask for help. This lessens frustration and emotional or physical outbursts.

Using Emotional Literacy in the class helps a great deal too. Rather than using "you haven't done this", try saying "how can we get going on this task, shall we break it down?" or "I was hoping we would all have started by now." The response is always more positive. The children will look around to help those who haven't begun; they begin to work step by step or look for an adult if they need help.

An important thing to remember is that this skill may take time to develop in a child with ADHD. So the idea of sharing feelings should be promoted and repeated within the class. A child with ADHD may find it hard to express his feelings freely. He may even have specific emotional issues depending on his circumstances and you may need to discuss this with his psychologist.

Emotional Literacy is about understanding your emotions and acting on them. Once a child can recognise an emotion, this allows you to introduce anger management strategies, relaxation techniques and much more.

Encourage the child to reward himself verbally. Advise him of his good behaviour and ask him how he feels. This raises self-esteem and gives the child a sense of pride. In the future you can also extend this to cover longer tasks.

By learning and applying these techniques in the classroom, a child's emotional development can be nurtured.

Case Study

While working in an Aided Primary School, I worked one-on-one with a child with ADHD for three months before his Emotional Literacy began to develop.

Previously he would rarely speak to others and would physically erupt if he became frustrated. After discussing basic emotions, we talked about frustration and he described it as a tense feeling 'like holding my breath'. I advised that if it felt like when he holds his breath, he should be sure to breathe deeply and calmly when he felt like that and raise

his hand to let me know. He said he did not want to raise his hand in front of the class, so we agreed that as a calming technique he would breathe deeply and count to ten inside his head (and move his head from side to side as he counted). This way I knew the child was frustrated and needed attention (via the physical signal) and he had a way to calm down at the same time. It took a long time to get to that point, but it was a real breakthrough for him and me.

Selena Ledgerton Cooper

Coaching

We know that children with ADHD need support on an emotional and behavioural level. They may be medicated and have an educational or behavioural support plan, but you are the most important facilitator for their learning, to ensure that they gain the most benefit.

The concept of Coaching was introduced and developed in this country by Dianne Zaccheo MSW. Coaching techniques used alongside Emotional Literacy provide enormous benefit to the child. Coaching is not a form of therapy. It is an outlook, an understanding between teacher and child, a connection and support system that can be life-changing.

Many forms of therapy have proved unsuccessful for children with ADHD as they only work on one level, but Coaching is a positive technique which nurtures a child, raises self-esteem and supports his emotions and behaviour.

How does it work?

The idea is to envisage yourself as a coach. Coaches instruct and practise new behaviours with you. They support you while you are in the process and cheer you on when you do well. Coaching offers an opportunity for better achievement through skill development, practice and encouragement.

Children with ADHD experience many frustrations. Time in relation to workload is an important one. Some children may feel the work is too difficult to complete in the time given, while others feel overwhelmed as the task seems too much or too long. These feelings can prevent the child from even starting a task, yet are not necessarily an indication of whether he has the skill to complete it.

Many children with ADHD are high achievers. They have the mental ability to complete the work, but they become frustrated because the work set is too easy or is not flexible enough. The task may not be suited to their learning style or offered in small comprehensible sections. Longer tasks can easily be broken down into chunks, with discussion times or reading groups allocated in between. It is easy to cause a child with ADHD to clam up because the workload is too overwhelming. The perception of the task can block its completion.

The Coaching techniques you use can help eliminate the negative feelings a child may have. They can also be added to your IEP or IBP as 'additional support offered'. The idea is to create a mutual agreement between you and the child which works towards effective change: a better attitude, new skills, and increased self-confidence.

As a coach you will understand the issues that come with ADHD and you can work effectively with the child to improve his skills and results. You can begin by helping the child to identify negative habits and the use of negative language. Discuss the positives and use the 'getting to know you' book to demonstrate all the fantastic things he can achieve and likes to do. Encourage him to use positive language about himself. Demonstrate this by emphasising his good points and how well he works. Reinforce this by creating a reward system and be sure to give praise verbally. Body language is important. Drop to his eye level when speaking, be open with regard to your gestures and maintain eye contact.

Talk to him, observe him and discover how he likes to learn. Tailor sessions so that he can be included in the class and take part, while avoiding possible triggers. Offer sessions that are split into shorter segments and provide a range of media to prevent boredom. When you introduce the lesson it is important to describe it in short understandable sentences. Perhaps draw a mind map or write bullet points so a child can take it step by step. To be a good coach, remember the most important tool - a smile!

It is all about breaking that initial barrier when the task is set, before frustration kicks in. Keep the child motivated to continue with the knowledge that he can succeed. You are raising his self-esteem by offering encouragement, telling him that he can do it and rewarding him when he does.

> *"A coach will always encourage you to be the best that you can be, because first and foremost, he is deeply invested in your success. The Coaching relationship is meant to be an equal partnership, designed to educate and empower both the coach and the child. Coaching as a technique can result in a real transformation of the self, helping to eliminate the most common ADHD problems, which are: Personal Achievement, Personal Perception, and Interpersonal Skills."*
>
> Dianne Zaccheo MSW.

Using Coaching techniques along with Emotional Literacy is of great benefit to children with ADHD. Introduce Emotional Literacy first, as this can help them share their feelings (which will support decisions on Coaching strategies). When children are told they can achieve and are encouraged to do so by someone who understands them, they can shine.

Case Study

A boy with ADHD (7 years) was really falling behind in class. He was unable to work independently and had problems fitting in with his peers.

He was often rejected by his friends because of his impulsive and aggressive behaviour. Pupils in his class would complain to staff and parents that he was breaking their things and being disruptive. The boy could not complete his work in school nor could he do homework. His mother described a daily battle at home (with crying, fits and screaming) just to get the homework done. The parents were frustrated and becoming exhausted as the child had seen numerous professionals and had been prescribed many forms of medication. The school had tried to accommodate this child, but was now concerned for the other pupils as his outbursts were becoming more frequent.

The boy would come home from school tearful and exhausted, he did not want to go to school the next day as he believed no one liked him. He would often take his anger out on his younger brother at home. Following the referral I examined the reports from his school and doctor and met with all the relevant professionals and parents. When it came to meeting the child, I thought it best not to be 'yet another professional he had to see', as this can be intimidating and can make the child feel as if there's something wrong with him. I joined the class and read everyone a story as a way of introduction. I remained with the class during lunch and observed

and when we took a look at his artwork, I was able to praise his work and gain trust. We talked about his perception and experiences in school, including his worries and fears. The boy articulated the same concerns about himself that all of the adults in his life had expressed.

He was painfully aware that he was slower at reading, couldn't spell words, had difficulty working for any length of time and that he sometimes couldn't control himself or the volume of his voice. He knew that he was out of step developmentally in terms of social engagement, team play and playing games. Eventually I told him I would like to help and I asked his permission to meet with his teachers and parents on his behalf. He was very keen for me to get started. I promised him that I would help to improve his academic experience (with his help) and we could make adjustments and changes that would allow him to enjoy school.

On getting to know him, I found that he loved learning, especially history. He had various collections of stamps, coins and soldiers and when I visited his home we really connected around his strengths rather than his weaknesses. This is the beginning of coaching... to get to know the child respectfully, to champion his strengths, advocate for his needs, encourage him to enjoy learning, and support him in positive and creative ways to enhance every aspect of the environment until he feels he can succeed.

Dianne Zaccheo MSW.

Social Issues and Bullying

A child with ADHD has a social vision of himself that is developed at school. Being unhappy at school will reflect on his whole life. School is where he learns to build relationships. It is one of the first places where he will develop different groups of friends, experience different cultures and learn to interact with adults other than parents.

Many children with ADHD have difficulties making friends because of their behaviour. Some children may believe they have little in common with a child with ADHD, whereas others may be fearful or intimidated by his behaviour. It is important that a child with ADHD has plenty of opportunity to talk about his interests while with his peers, so that others have an opportunity to see past his behaviour.

Social connections are problematic for children with ADHD as they can find positive and negative signals

difficult to understand. They may be unaware if a conversation is going well and feel intimidated. If sarcasm or humour is used, they can misinterpret the joke. It can be an upsetting time, as social connections develop self-esteem and make children happy.

Sadly, many children with ADHD will make friends because of their behaviour. Children are drawn to a child they find unusual and 'funny'. Unfortunately the novelty wears off when the ADHD child spoils their game or has a tantrum and his new friends suddenly disappear.Fortunately most children with ADHD do make friends. Regardless of their behaviour, their charm and personality shine through and connections are made. Other relationships can be developed further by offering them information on out-of-school groups and clubs, where children can gain vital life experience.

Some children with ADHD may connect with younger children. This is not a problem and can be a benefit as they develop essential social skills during play. Younger children are learning how to interact with others too and the children can build their relationships together.

When you are on duty outside or when taking circle time, take the opportunity to introduce team games. Encourage all the children to interact and feel unified. Praise both winners and losers and promote self-worth. During lessons you can also 'buddy up' the children for certain tasks and change the buddies every day. This way the child can get to know all the children in the class, which can help build relationships.

With regard to family relationships, you may think that what happens at home is the parents' business. While this is true, the parents should contact you via the communication book or phone if there are any problems that may affect the child in school. Arguments in the morning can affect the whole day and a parent leaving home can shatter the child. Issues with siblings can also be damaging, especially if the children attend the same school, as the argument may escalate in school.

Bullying

As social connections can be difficult and misunderstood, it is important to be aware of bullying. A child with ADHD may bully other children, as he feels isolated, in need of attention and is aware his behaviour is intimidating. Other children may bully a child with ADHD as he is an easy target. A child with ADHD may also be bullied because of his behaviour. I have worked with many children who were bullied because other children saw them as irritating and annoying.

Battling bullying is difficult, but you can help by being as approachable as possible and advising the child to come to you with any problems. If the child is distant or upset, it may be time for a one-on-one. If he has anger issues or violent tendencies himself, he may need to be supervised from a distance to ensure he is not bullying others.

Medication

It is important as a teacher, teaching assistant or practitioner, to understand the various medications available for children with ADHD. These are increasing (and changing) all the time, though it is essential that you are aware of the various options. Usually a child will be prescribed medication when his behaviour is severe, he is disruptive, extremely hyperactive or has major concentration issues. It is used to help control symptoms, not control behaviour.

Medication will usually be recommended after academic, emotional or behavioural support has been put in place. This is because doctors and psychologists will normally use observations from assessments and schools to help find the most suitable drug. When a child is prescribed a particular medication, you should research it in detail. Learn about any specific side-effects and confirm the dosage if the child needs to take it in school. Ensure it is locked in the school's medicine cabinet and only given to the child at the appropriate time by you or an authorised adult. Log each medication in line with your school's policy, be sure to document any reactions the child may have and advise the parents and relevant professionals. Being singled out from a crowd can trigger a child with ADHD, so be as discreet as possible when administering the child's medication.

Medications prescribed to treat ADHD are usually psychostimulants, though tricyclic antidepressants are also used. Don't be put off by the medical jargon. Psychostimulants alter the levels of natural chemicals in the brain, which may be out of balance in ADHD children. In some children, stimulant medications can create a window of opportunity where a child's concentration and focus improves. After taking medication a child may find it easier to engage and could also be more receptive to strategies and support offered. Tasks can be less intimidating, instructions can be more comprehensible and communication may be easier, though it is important to note that medications have different effects and results with each child.

Common side effects of these medications may include wakefulness at night and a reduced appetite, though the parents and GP will be aware of this and the child's weight should be checked regularly. If the child needs to be medicated at school, check with both parents and doctor to see if the medication can be given with lunch, as this can sometimes help with any side effects.

Should a medicated child experience any of these more concerning side- effects, you should notify his parents and advise them to contact their GP: nausea, stomach ache, anxiety, tearfulness, irritability, over-focusing (staring and quiet), nervousness, headaches. dizziness, drowsiness and twitching.

If there are any other symptoms that concern you, you should again notify the parents immediately and advise them to contact their GP for a review.

When a child is on medication, his prescription will be reviewed regularly by his GP and psychologist. The dosage will be checked and any revisions made depending on their behaviour. The child will also require annual medication breaks. You should ask the parents to notify you of any dosage changes or if the child is on a break, so you may prepare for this and note it in your observations. This will show if there are any significant changes to discuss in the next review meeting. Changes in medication should also be documented on the child's IEP or IBP.

If a child responds well to medication, it can be a great help as the support strategies you offer will be easier for the child to absorb. It gives you a chance to offer him the social and emotional tools he needs to manage his behaviour. In turn he is more likely to be able to handle his behaviour, even when he takes a medication break.

Many medications can help some children a great deal. Some can calm a child who may be aggressive or hyperactive, but none is a solution to the problem. ADHD is a disorder. It is neurological, physical, emotional and behavioural and therefore it should be treated on all levels. Medication may help or it may not. Consider these points when working with a medicated child:

1. Following diagnosis, parents, in consultation with doctors, should decide whether they would like their child to try medication. It is the responsibility of a trained psychologist, specialist or doctor to suggest suitable medications. Take care! Anything you say to parents prior to that meeting may influence their decision to medicate their child. They may even request a drug based on your discussion. If parents ask you about possible medications for their child, advise them that every child is different and refer them to their GP.

2. Many medications will calm a child who has ADHD and some may even aid concentration, but that doesn't mean that other symptoms subside. It is still your responsibility to support him emotionally, physically and with regard to his behaviour. It is more than likely that he will still require an IBP or IEP and if he already has one, it should be revised to include details of his medication and then continued. You should also detail any improvements, attitude to work, and changes in behaviour or focus, as this will help you and other professionals to chart the difference since the child was medicated. Hold regular meetings to discuss any changes with the relevant professionals, the head, parents and child.

3. It is important that you are as honest as possible and do not give the parents or child false hope. In this situation anything you say can be misunderstood. If a family has tried everything and you say "it will help" instead of "it may help", that becomes something to hope for. Parents will look to you for knowledgeable answers, but if the medication is not successful then they may feel that you were misleading. When a child has been prescribed medication, parents always ask if it will work. Many children think this is a magic pill and parents may have heard that another child with ADHD recovered completely. You must provide honest but tactful answers. Tell a child that his medication may help with some things, but we need to keep to our goals so we can work on the other things. With parents, say that "some medications may help some children, though some do not. We will think positively and continue to work together to help the child." Also let them know about any changes or improvements.

This section is not intended to dismiss the idea of medication. Many children respond well to it and their behaviour and concentration improves. Many texts over-sensationalise the idea of medication and you need practical advice that is realistic.

Rewards and sanctions

Ask the children to help you decide rewards and sanctions. This can give them a sense of responsibility, it can raise self-esteem and if they incur a sanction they will be less confrontational.

Reward schemes work best if a child can build up points or stickers to reach a reward (a certificate in assembly for example), but a long-term reward is not an incentive for a child with ADHD. It is a good idea to introduce additional rewards which run alongside this central scheme.

As a child with ADHD needs on-the-spot rewards and instant recognition, the other children may feel resentful as the ADHD child is receiving continuous positive attention. Although rewards are positive, an ADHD child can feel singled out if you treat him differently. Try to reward all the children in the same way, but feel free to vary the rewards.

Rewards can include: a DVD to watch (class reward), free time at the end of the week (class reward), additional playtime (class reward), stickers, a choice of activities, time on the PC.

You can mark on the class timetable the days on which the children can earn each reward. Tell them that fantastic behaviour could earn a bonus sticker, even when it is not a sticker day. Be sure to explain the scheme to the whole class and include all the children. Make the details clear and state why they will receive a reward or a punishment. When the children receive a sanction, they can be referred to the golden rule sheet so they can understand the consequence of any errors.

Punishment is not always necessary. A child deserves a warning and the opportunity to turn his behaviour around. All systems suggested here do just that. Schools should have a positive behaviour policy in place and teachers should be encouraged to reward positive behaviour and ignore minor disruptions. This way the children understand that poor behaviour does not get any attention. Children should come to learn that when they are good they receive attention from the teacher and a reward. When giving a sanction you should be direct, explain the reason for the sanction, but give as little attention as possible.

All children are different, so they should be rewarded for different (as well as similar) things. If a child is normally messy and cleans up, he should be rewarded, whereas a child who is always tidy (but noisy) can be rewarded for sitting quietly. Identify elements of behaviour that a child has improved on and reward them. Children should also be praised for being courteous, following the rules, having pride in their appearance and for being punctual.

Children deserve a chance to moderate their actions. Try a traffic light board as a behaviour system. Place three large coloured discs on the wall (green, amber and red) and have all the children's names on green. If a child begins to behave poorly or starts to throw a tantrum, give as little attention as possible and put their name on the amber light. This is a warning. Advise that if they reach the red marker they will have to have a time out (or whatever you sanction you have in place). If a child reaches the amber light and turns his behaviour round be sure to put him straight back on the green and give him lots of praise and attention. Also, remember to reset all the names every morning, as a new day should mean a fresh start for every child. This system is both positive and empowering, as the child can affect the outcome by his own actions.

For very young children, adapt the system with a smiley, straight and sad face or a sun, a cloud and rain. You can use laminated photos of the children's faces if they are unable to read their names. Punishments should only be used if the child has not turned his behaviour round and he lands on the red circle, sad face or rain cloud.

Sanctions should be age-specific, though here are some suggestions: remove a child's sticker from the board (he can earn this back), move him from his group to a separate table, lose time from playtime or lunchtime play, lose an activity, lose allocated free time, lose PC time.

For more severe behaviours the child: may be sent to stand alone, may be sent to another teacher (accompanied), may be sent to the deputy or head (accompanied) or parents may be contacted.

Continuous negative or violent behaviour can result in suspension or exclusion.

Behaviours resulting in rewards or punishments should be noted in the parent-teacher communication book. If major problems persist, the child may need referring to his child psychologist for further consultation or a medication check.

Relaxation and anger management techniques

Children with ADHD can have different responses to each technique, so feel free to try different techniques to see which works for them. These techniques can be noted on the child's IEP or IBP and any results and observations should be recorded.

- Take several slow and deep breaths;
- Take a deep breath in, squeeze your finger as you exhale. Repeat with all fingers;
- Sit quietly with legs crossed, drop your shoulders and roll your head for five counts in each direction as you breathe deeply and slowly;
- Raise your arms above your head slowly and breathe in, lower your arms slowly and breathe out;
- Play music in the class;
- Provide a chill-out and time-out area;
- Offer headphones so a child can listen to relaxing music;
- Lead by example – stay calm;
- Encourage emotional literacy. A child is less likely to become angry if he can discuss his feelings;
- Practise strategies such as 'stop and think' with the child;
- Hold one nostril closed and breathe in, swap nostrils and breathe out. Breathe slowly and concentrate on each breath;
- Encourage the child to self-manage. When he feels angry he can recognise it and say "I'm angry, I need to go and calm down." This doesn't need to be said out loud;
- Introduce a weekly chill-out session with a relaxation CD or DVD (watch it yourself first to ensure it is suitable).

During relaxation techniques children should remain as quiet as possible and blank their minds. If the technique is used as a form of anger management to calm a child, he should be encouraged to use the time to review what happened and think of possible solutions.

This is my own group relaxation:

"Lie down, close your eyes, breathe deeply and relax. Imagine you are lying on a cloud and with each breath you sink deeper and deeper into the soft fluffy cloud. Deeper and deeper... (Pause and allow the children to breathe). Deeper and deeper... (Repeat four times) Now... you are completely relaxed, imagine a warm orange glow above your head. With each breath it warms and soothes, sending wonderful relaxing energy into your body, washing away all your stress. Slowly but surely the glow moves slowly across your head, it warms and relaxes your forehead, then your brow... it relaxes your eyes ...and warms your face. With every breath it takes away all the stress and tension of the day."

Were you relaxed? You can continue this so the orange glow moves down the body and relaxes all the muscles. On completion advise the children to open their eyes, sit up slowly, stretch and smile. They should remain sitting for a while before they stand.

Selena Ledgerton Cooper

Observation sheets for IBP or IEP

To create an Individual Education Plan (IEP) or an Individual Behaviour Plan (IBP), you must have information on how the child works in class. When planning strategies and care for the future you must first understand what the child needs, his triggers and how he responds in different learning environments. Thus you can create an appropriate action plan which encourages 'in-class' learning, avoids triggers, allows for flexibility and lists rewards, boundaries and consequences, all in the interest of the child.

Observation sheets, detailed notes and the 'getting to know you' book are valuable resources which

you can use during behaviour support and planning meetings. They can be referred to when drawing up a plan and they can also be offered as additional information for psychologists and professionals, during the statementing process, within the boundaries of data protection.

Log negative incidents in an observation book for each child. Important details such as dates and times should be included, as well as injuries, poor or threatening behaviour and the consequences the child received. His reactions during the incident should be noted, as well as how he responded to other children and staff members. These should be detailed notes as every incident can provide a mine of information about the child and any issues he may have. They can also be used during any investigations or if any injuries or self-harm occurs. Injuries should also be documented in the first aid book. All observation notes should be signed by any members of staff who were present during the incident and the observation book, along with any observation sheets and other personal details, should be stored in a locked filing cabinet at all times - preferably in a locked office. Documents should be signed in and signed out of this cabinet by an authorised member of staff. This responsibility is yours and is a legal requirement of the Data Protection Act.

Observation sheets can be completed by teachers who take the child throughout the day. These should also include qualified staff on duty during breaks and lunch. This is an important time, as many children respond differently when they are with their peers or in a more relaxed environment. Again, these sheets should be stored in line with data protection.

The reason for observations is often misunderstood. The main point of observing is to help the child. You are not just looking for what makes him kick off or run riot, you are looking for times when he is calm, moments when he focuses and the reasons why he does so. The positives can tell you more and the points to look for are listed on the Observation Sheet.

If you are aware of how well a child can work in specific environments, you can encourage and support this via your planning. Negative behaviours

and triggers can be listed on observation sheets if they occur, but the observation book is a more detailed resource for these incidents. Using the observation book for negative behaviour and using day-to-day observation sheets for the positive is a helpful strategy. If a negative incident occurs during the day, refer to it on the day-to-day sheet and provide detailed notes in the observation book. This way both sets of records are clear, thorough, and easy to follow.

The inside front cover of this booklet shows an example of an observation sheet, with additional note space and questions. The list of questions is quite detailed, but observation sheets can be simplified based on the child's behaviour and needs. You may wish to add these questions to the base of each sheet for your reference or review them at the end of the day and make notes.

Useful Contacts

Selena Ledgerton
Education & Childcare Consultant / Author
sledgin@hotmail.com

Adders   Online ADHD Support Group
The National Attention Deficit Disorder Information and Support Service
ADDISS, PO Box 340, Edgware, Middlesex HA8 9HL
http://www.adders.org info@addiss.co.uk

Brain Gym Courses
Contact your Local Education Authority to find courses in your area.

Dianne Zaccheo MSW
The Coaching Centre UK
http://zaccheotraining.com/index.php dzaccheo@hotmail.co.uk

Contact details correct in October 2007.